Abracadabra Violin

Book 2 – Piano accompaniments

James Alexander

A & C Black · London

Turkey in the straw *(Violin part: page 4)*

traditional
arr. B.C.T.

The wraggle taggle gypsies *(page 4)*

traditional
arr. J.S.

D.S. (no repeat) al Fine

In dulci jubilo *(page 6)*

14th century German
arr. J.S.

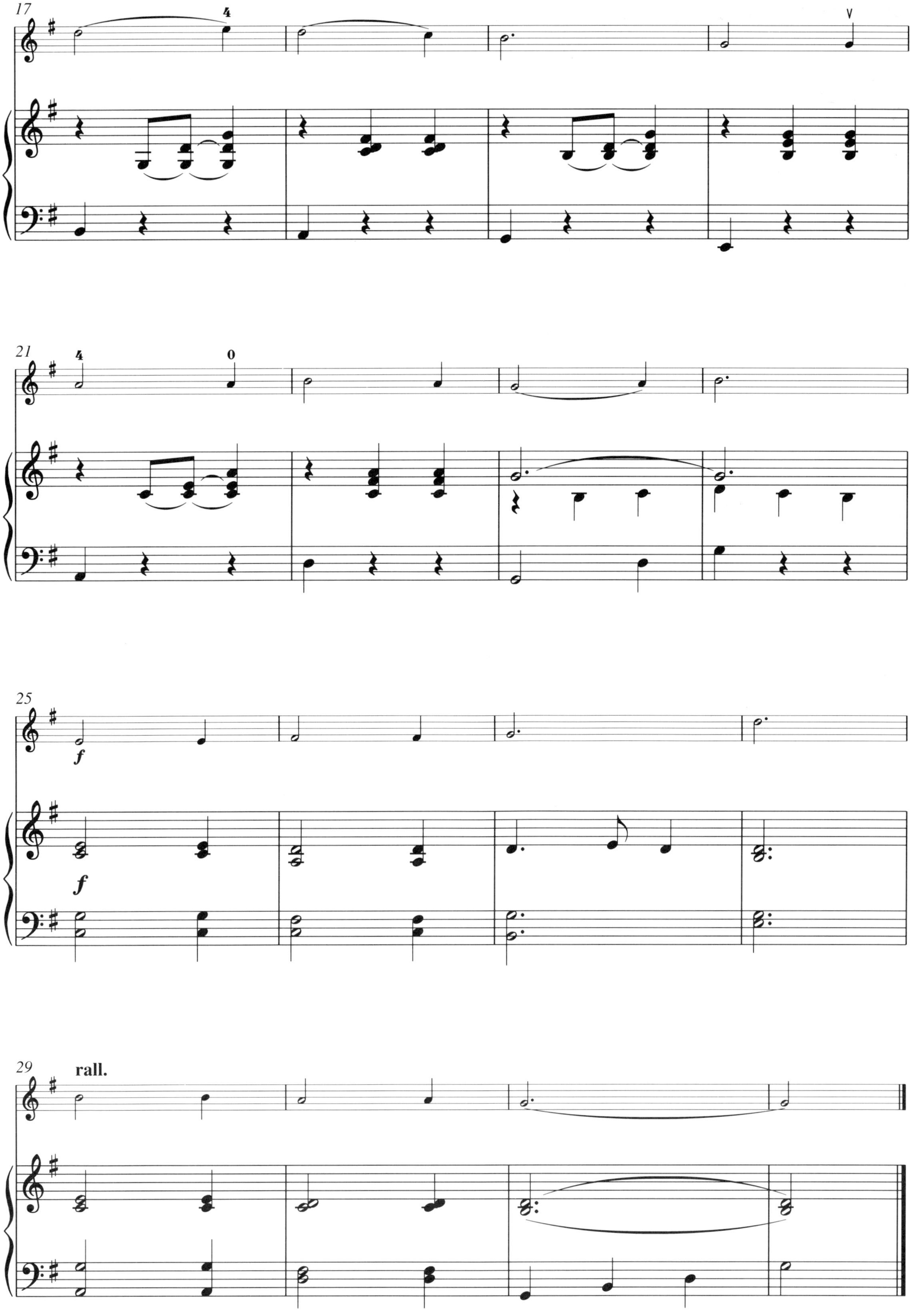
17
4
21
4
0
25
f
f
29
rall.

Down the green fields *(page 8)*

traditional
arr. B.C.T.

D.C. al Fine

Simple gifts *(page 10)*

Shaker melody
arr. J.A./B.C.T.

The wreck (round) *(page 10)*

Jan Holdstock
arr. J.S.

Un-der-neath the sea, Far a-way from land, That's where I will be, Shak-ing on the sand, Ratt-ling in my rig-ging Di-ther-ing on my deck, I'm just a ner - - vous wreck!

Tum balaika *(page 11)*

traditional
arr. J.S.

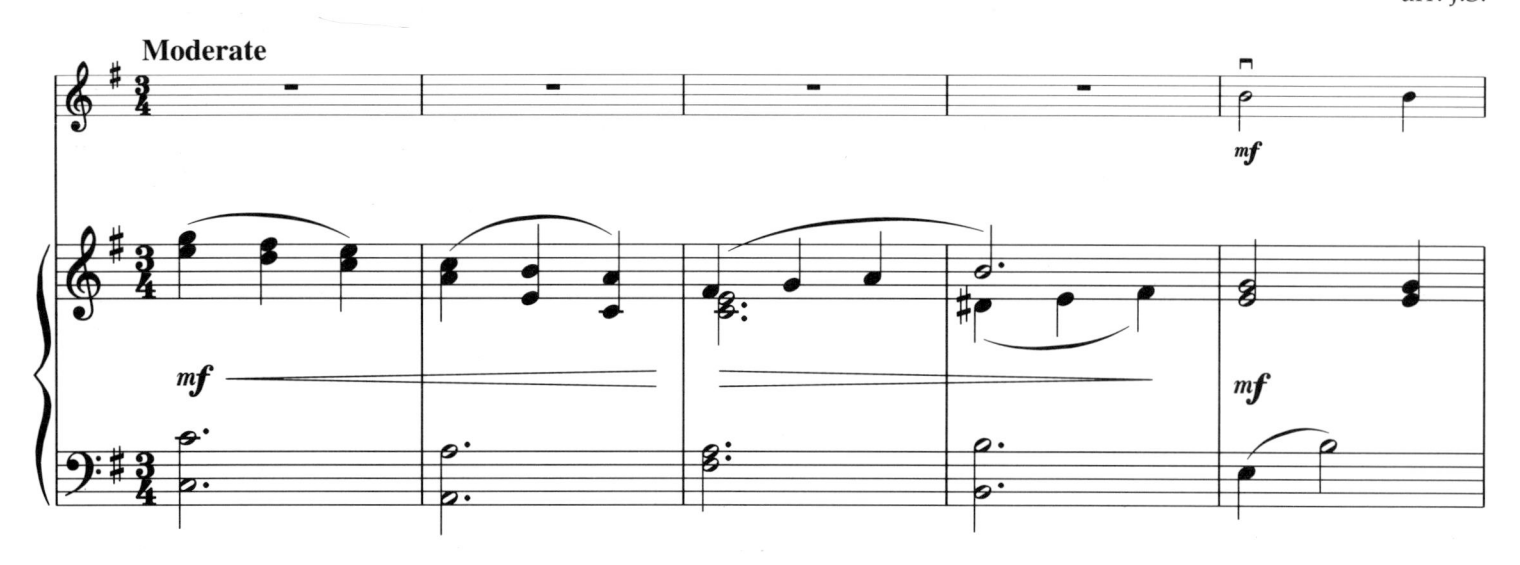

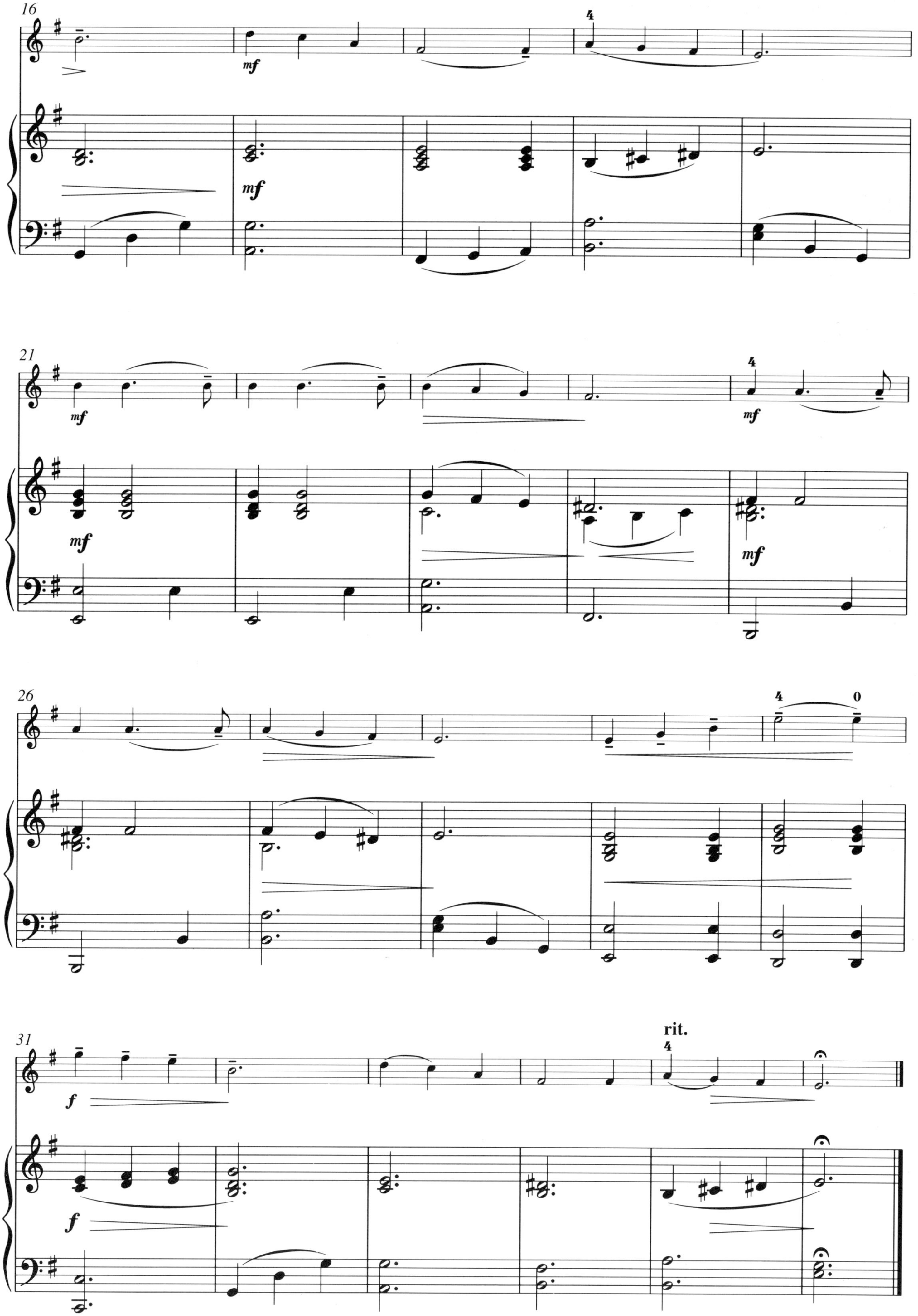
16
mf
mf
4
21
mf
mf
4
mf
mf
26
4
0
31
f
f
rit.
4

Theme and variations (page 12)
from *The 'Surprise' Symphony*

Haydn
arr. J.A./B.C.T.

13

The Mexican hat dance *(page 13)*

traditional
arr. B.C.T.

15

Greensleeves *(page 15)*

traditional
arr. J.S.

The jolly miller

traditional
arr. H.F./J.S.

Theme

Variations 1 - 4

Entr'acte from *Rosamunde* (No. 2) *(page 18)*

Schubert
arr. B.C.T.

Trumpet hornpipe *(page 19)*

traditional Irish
arr. B.C.T.

The animals went in two by two (page 20)

traditional
arr. J.S.

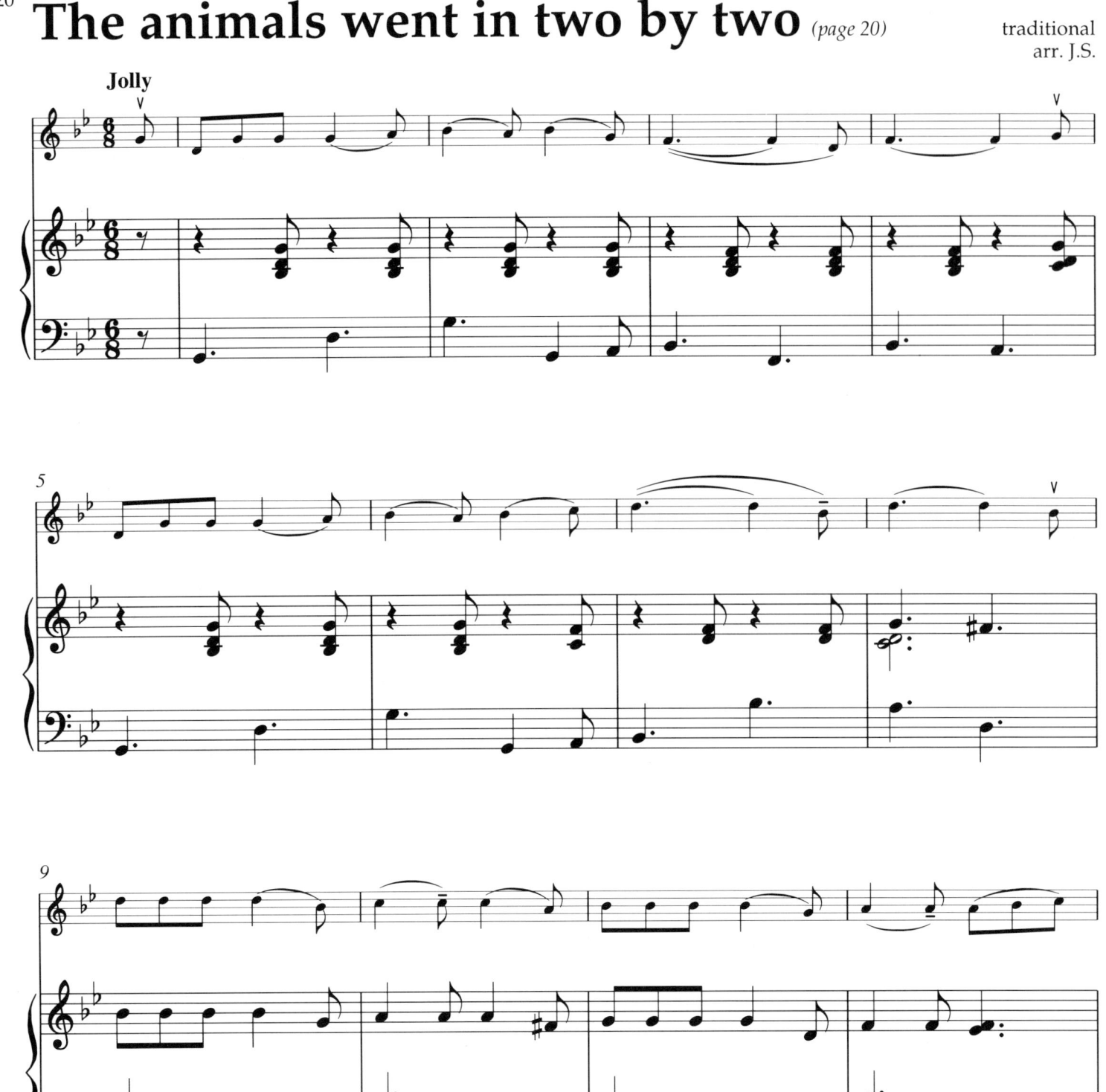

Jim Boulton's fancy *(page 21)*

Irish hornpipe
arr. B.C.T.

Idylle *Op. 30 No. 1* *(page 23)*

Wilhelm Dölb

Andantino

Hava nagila *(page 23)*

traditional Israeli
arr. J.S.

Bill Bailey, won't you please come home? *(page 25)*

traditional
arr. J.A./B.C.T.

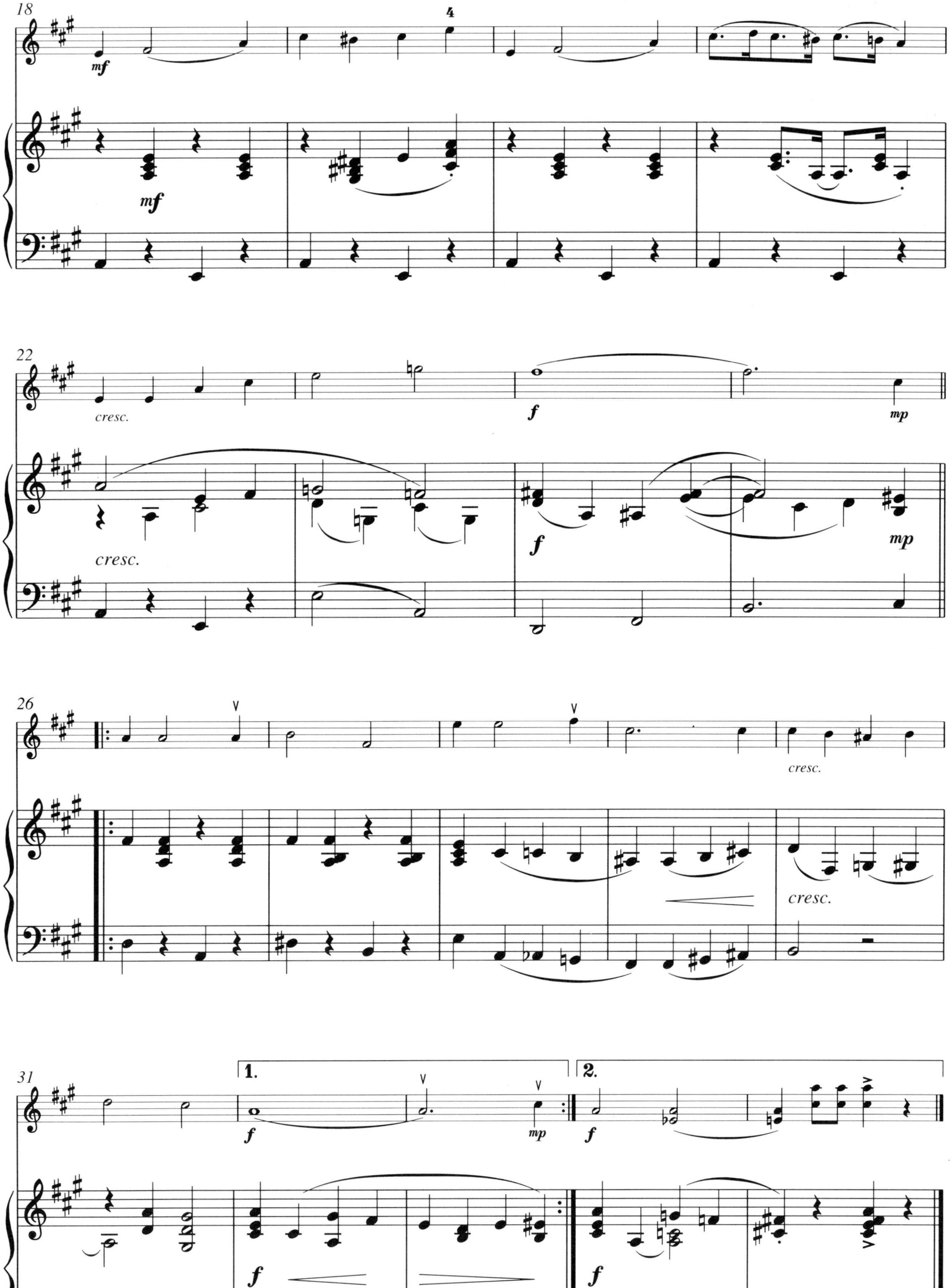
18
4
mf
mf
22
cresc.
cresc.
f
f
mp
mp
26
cresc.
cresc.
31
1.
f
f
mp
2.
f
f

Sailor's waltz *(page 26)*

J.A.
arr. B.C.T.

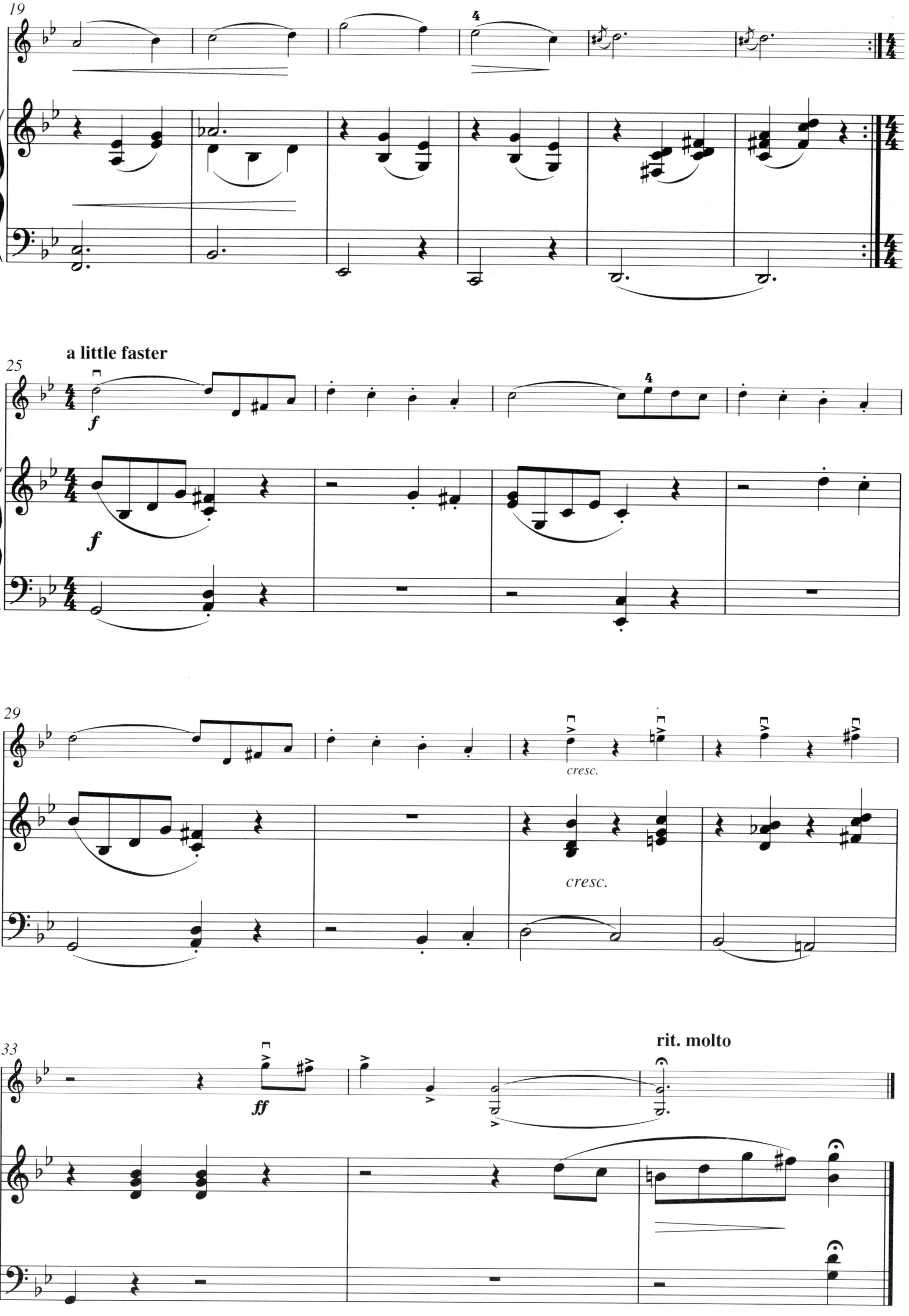
19
25
a little faster
f
f
29
cresc.
cresc.
33
ff
rit. molto

Morris dance *(page 27)*

W.C.Honeyman
arr.B.C.T.

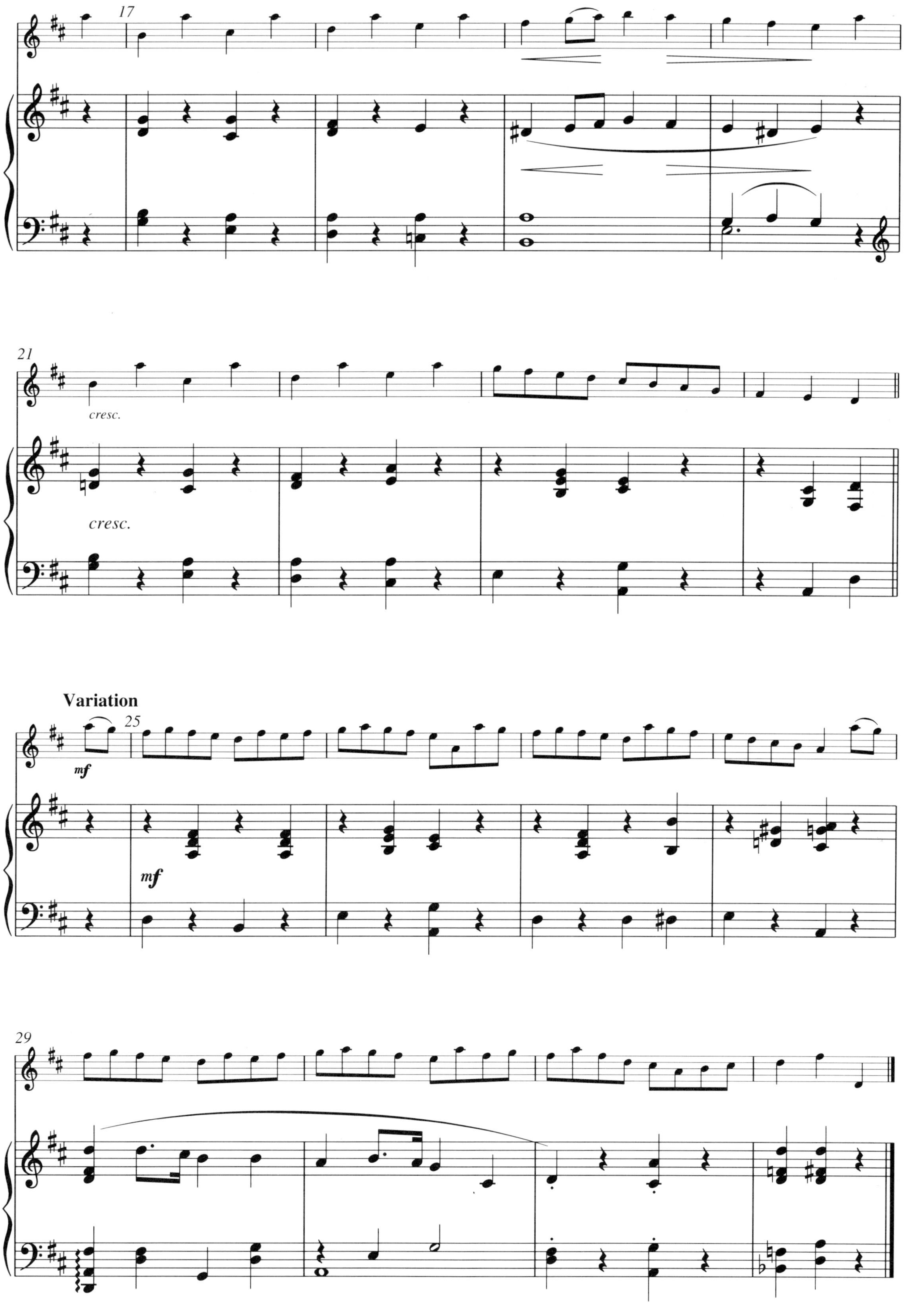
17
21
cresc.
cresc.
Variation
25
mf
mf
29

Amazing grace *(page 29)*

traditional
arr. J.S.

Cossack song *(page 29)*

traditional
arr. J.S.

Allegro moderato

La Cucaracha *(page 30)*

traditional
arr. B.C.T.

33

Strangers in the night *(page 31)*

Bert Kaempfert
arr. B.C.T.

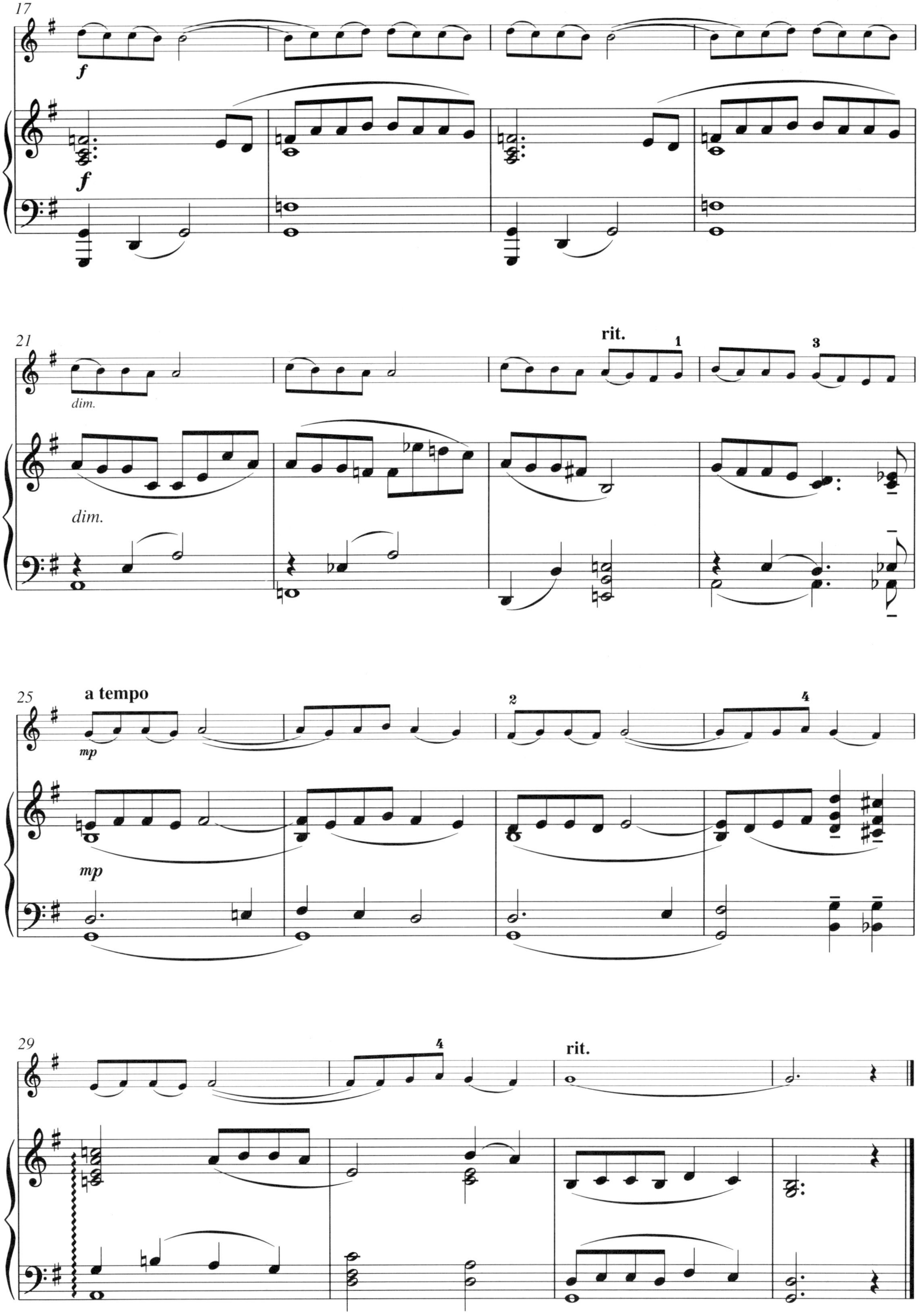
17
f
f
21
dim.
dim.
rit.
a tempo
mp
mp
29
rit.

Minuet from *Berenice* (page 32)

Handel
arr. B.C.T.

37

The mountains high *(page 33)*

Irish air
arr. B.C.T.

39

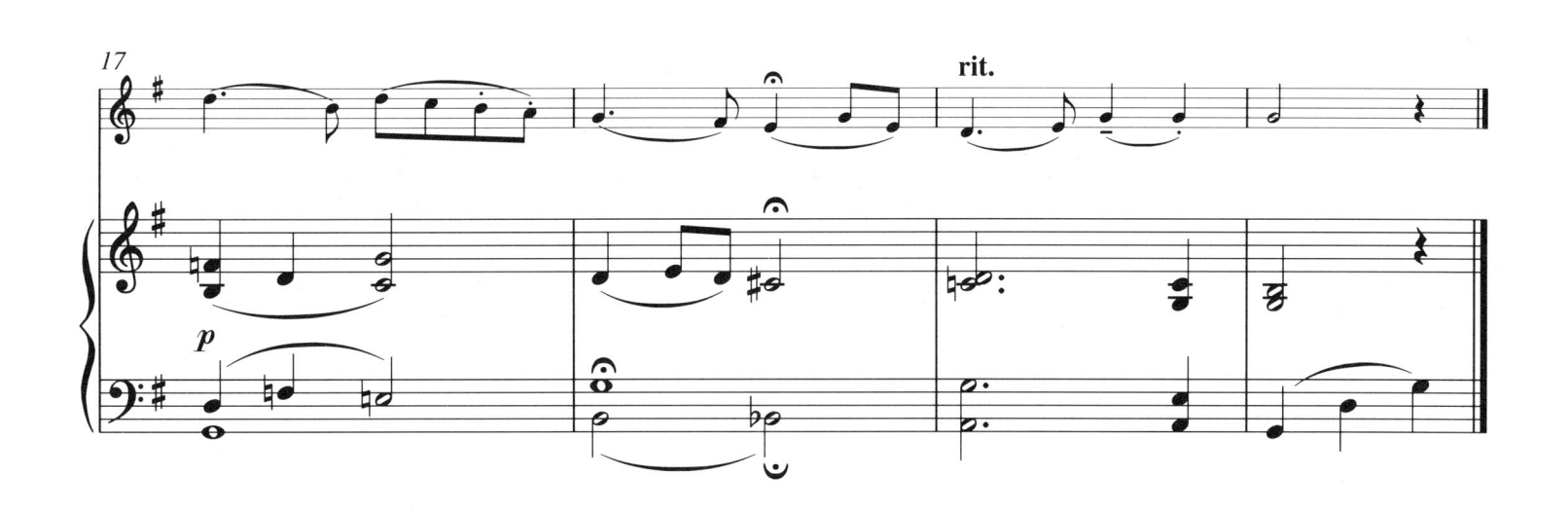

On wings of song *(page 34)*

Mendelssohn
arr. B.C.T.

13
mp
mp
16
p
decresc.
to Coda
poco rit.
19
1
p
22
sfz
2
dim.
dim.
25
D.S. al Coda
p

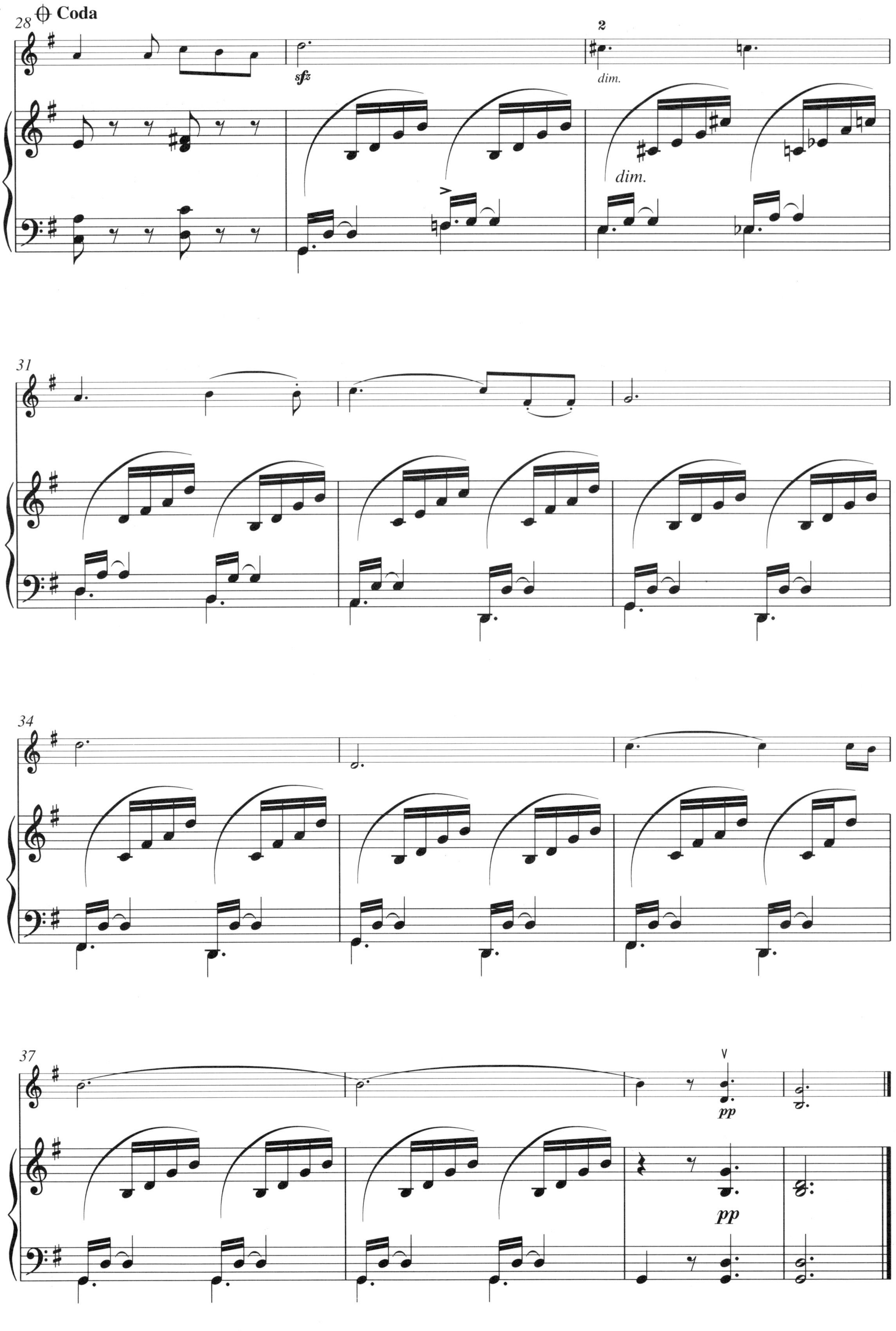
28
Coda
sfz
2
dim.
dim.
31
34
37
pp
pp

Theme from *Bergerac* (page 36)

George Fenton
arr. B.C.T.

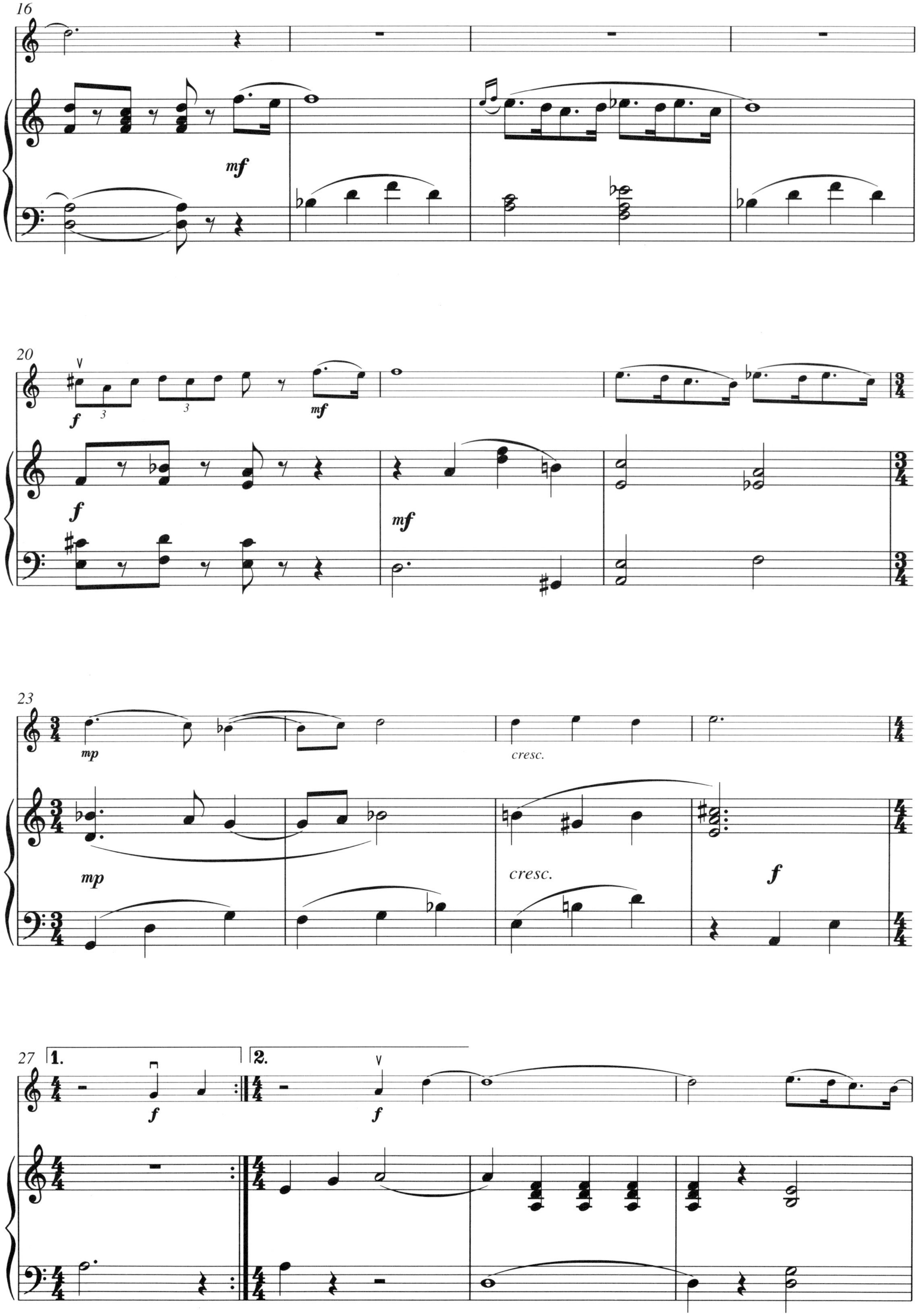
16
mf
20
f
mf
f
mf
23
mp
mp
cresc.
cresc.
f
27
1.
f
2.
f

45

Londonderry air *(page 37)*

traditional Irish
arr. B.C.T.

The lonely goatherd (page 38)

Richard Rodgers
arr. B.C.T.

Moderately fast

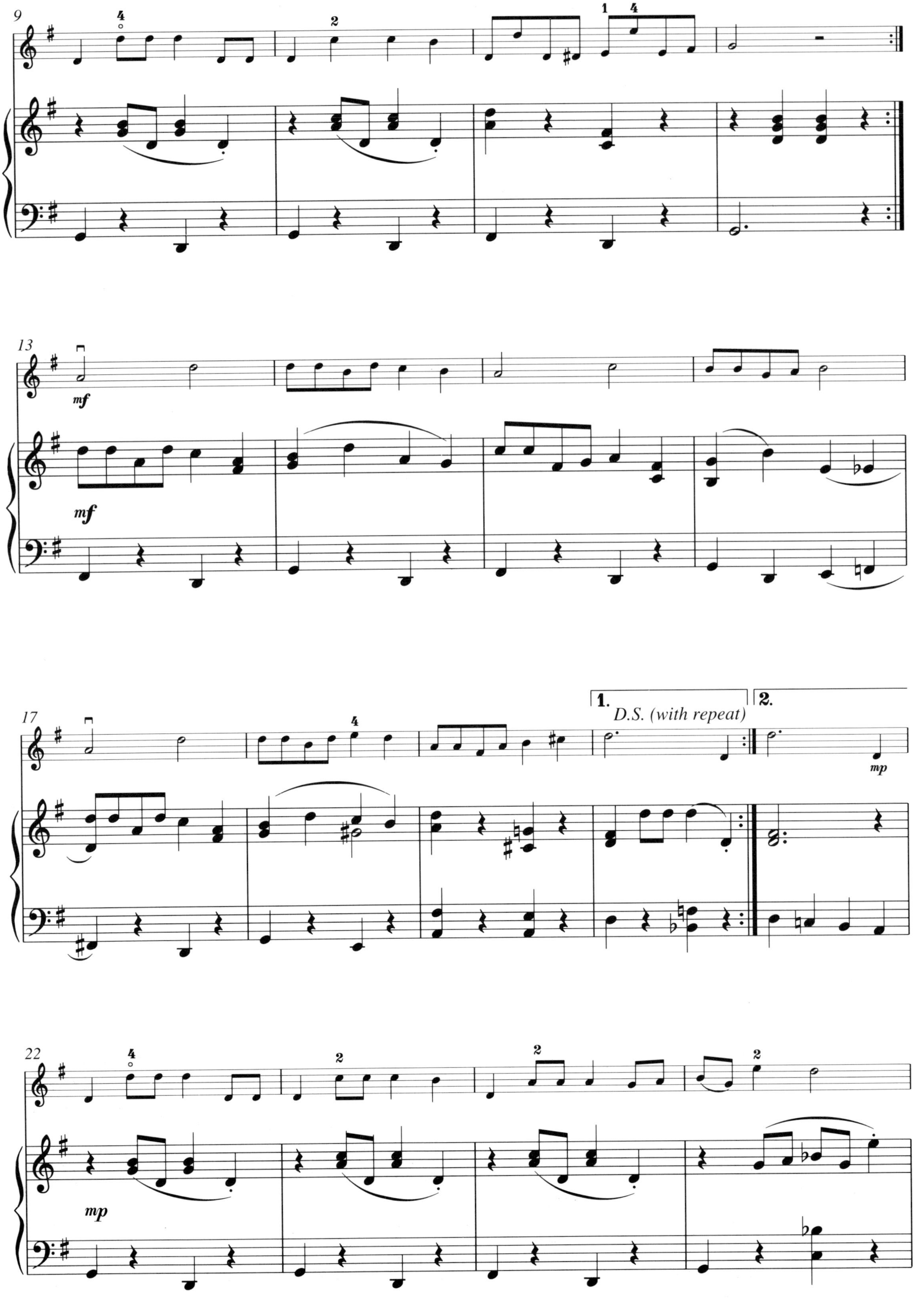
9
13
mf
mf
17
1.
D.S. (with repeat)
2.
mp
22
mp

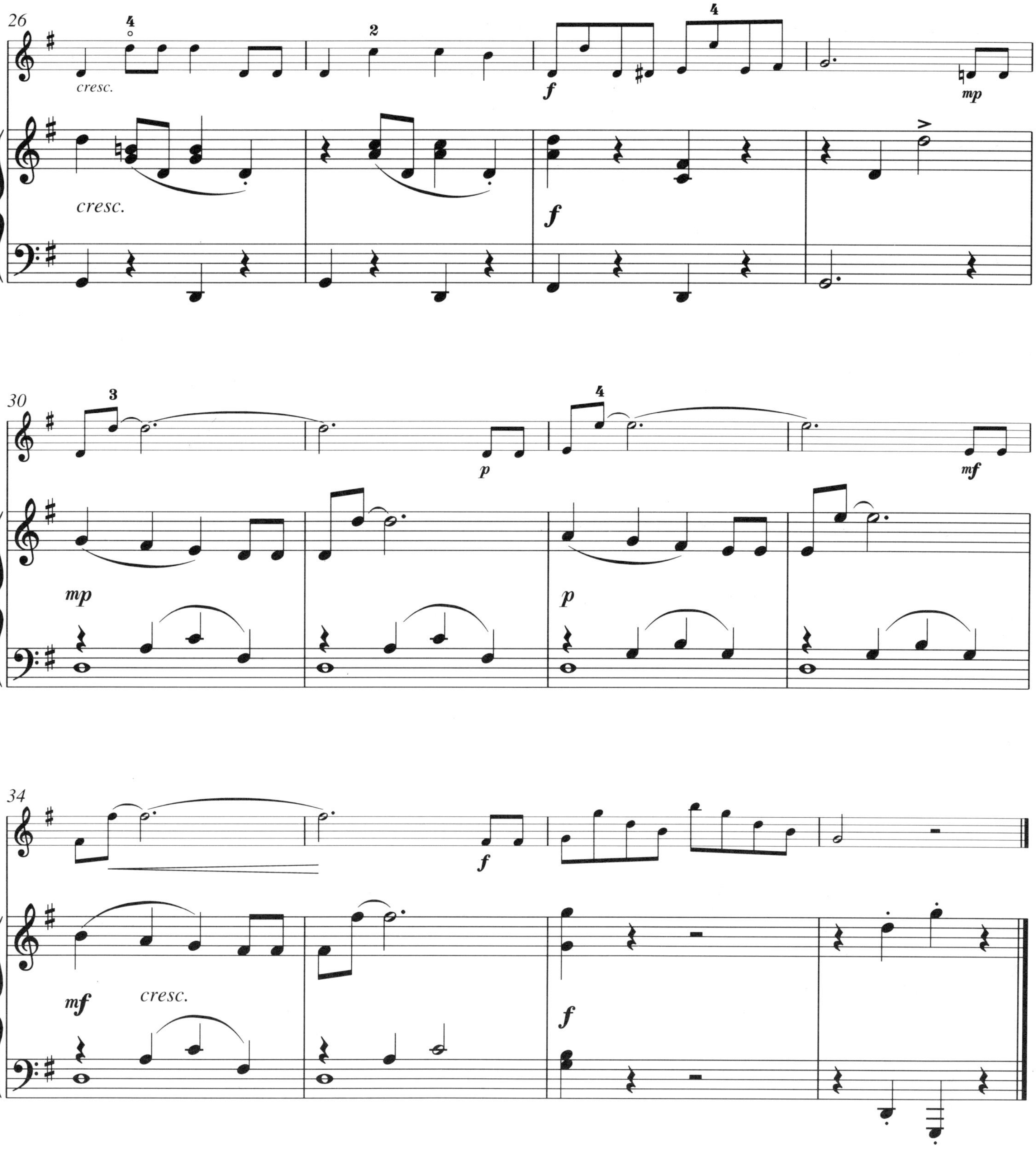
26
cresc.
cresc.
30
34
cresc.

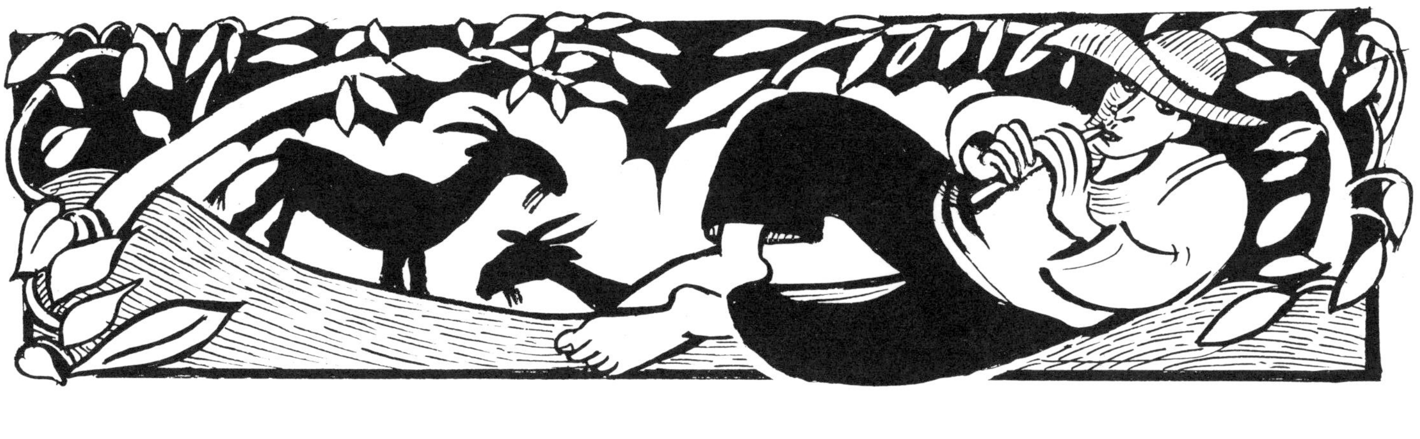

Agatha Christie's Poirot (page 39)

Christopher Gunning
arr. B.C.T.

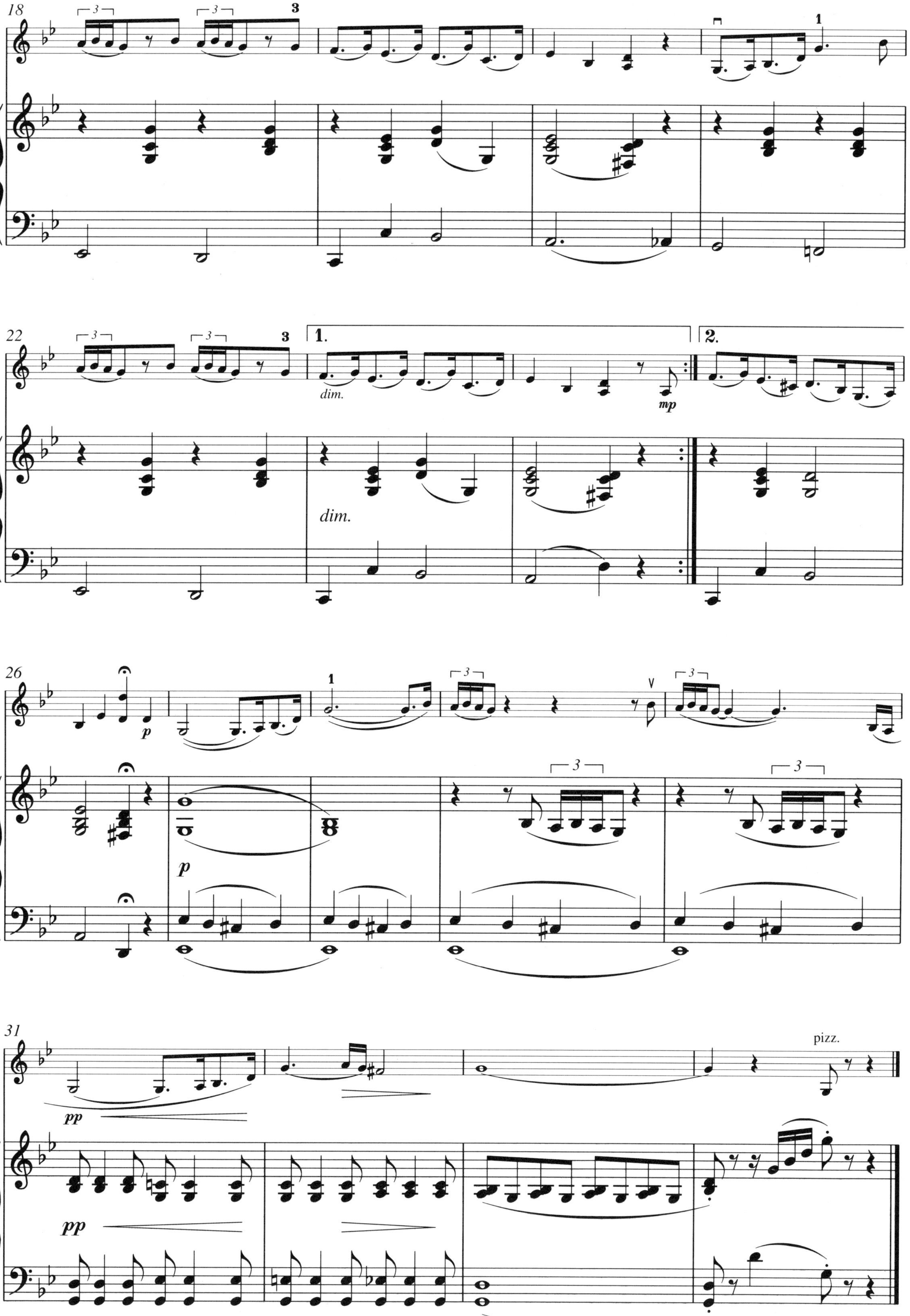
18
22
1.
2.
dim.
mp
26
p
31
pp
pizz.

Waltz from *Swan Lake* (page 40)

Tchaikovsky
arr. B.C.T.

Tempo di valse

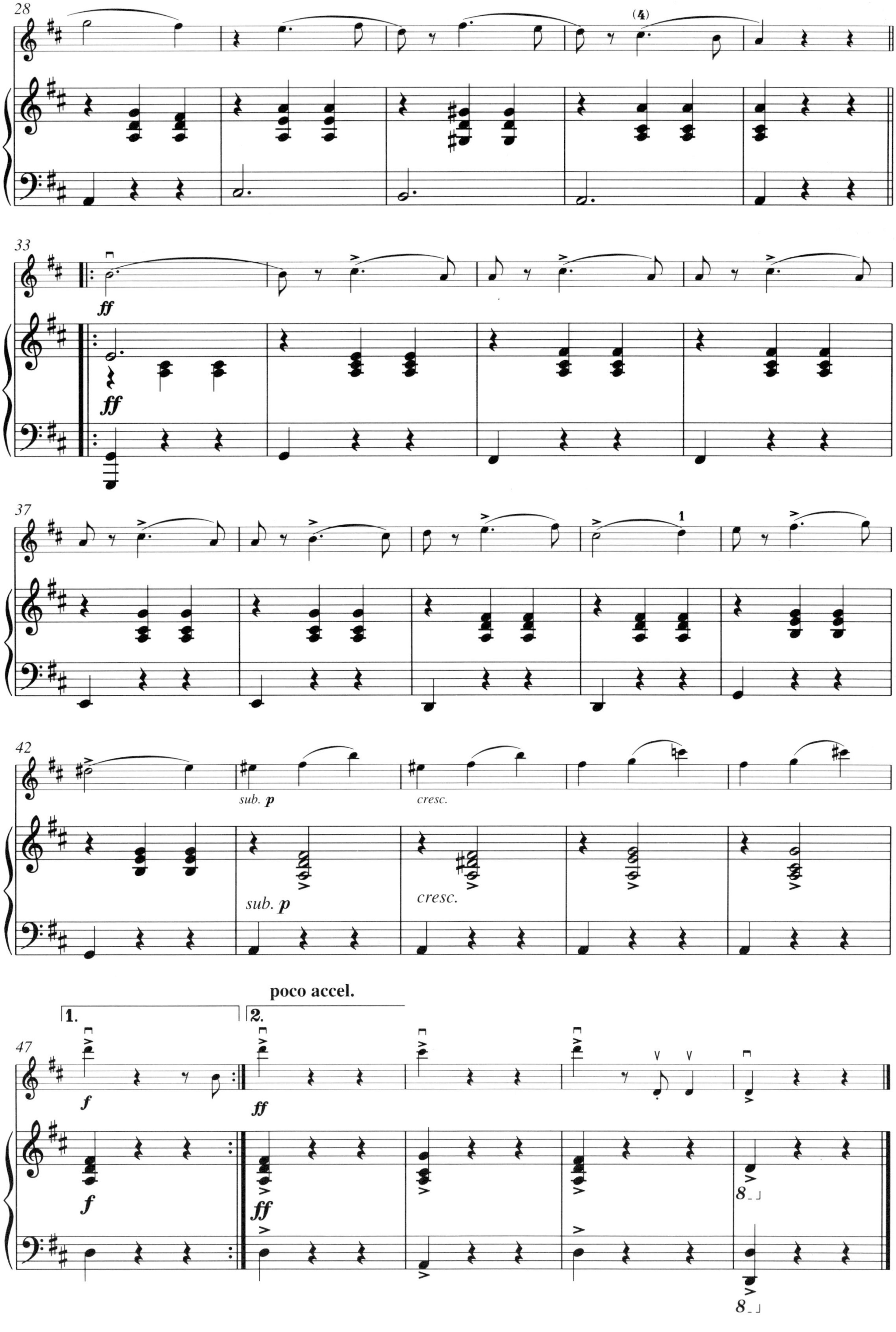

ff
sub. p
cresc.
poco accel.
1.
2.
f
ff

Siciliano from *Album for the Young* (page 41)

Schumann
arr. B.C.T.

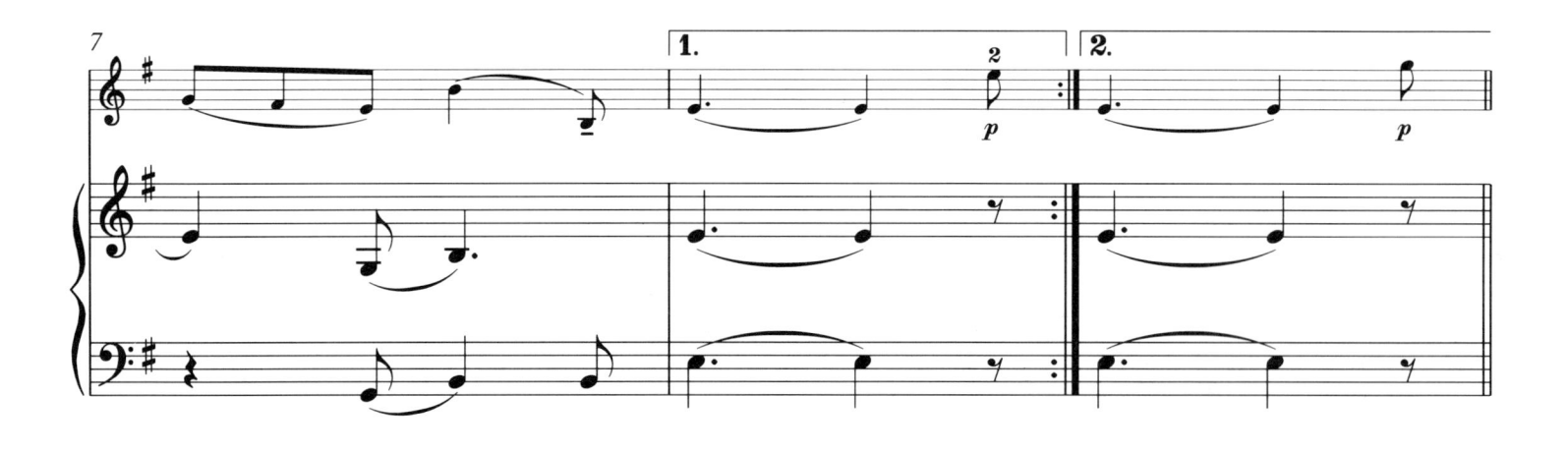

Gently and sweetly

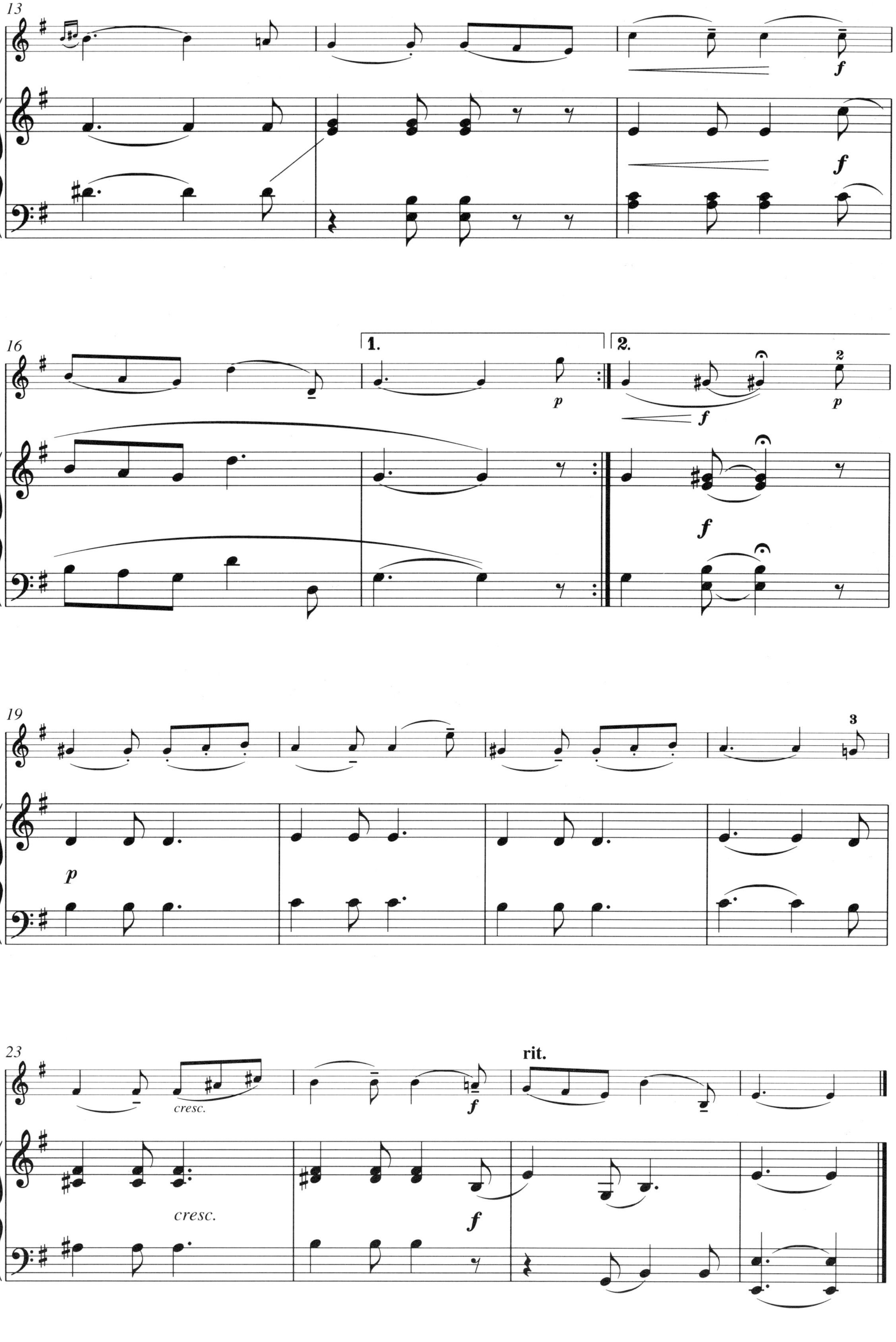
13
f
f
16
1.
2.
p
f
p
f
19
p
23
rit.
cresc.
f
cresc.
f

Swinging star *(page 42)*

J.A.
arr. B.C.T.

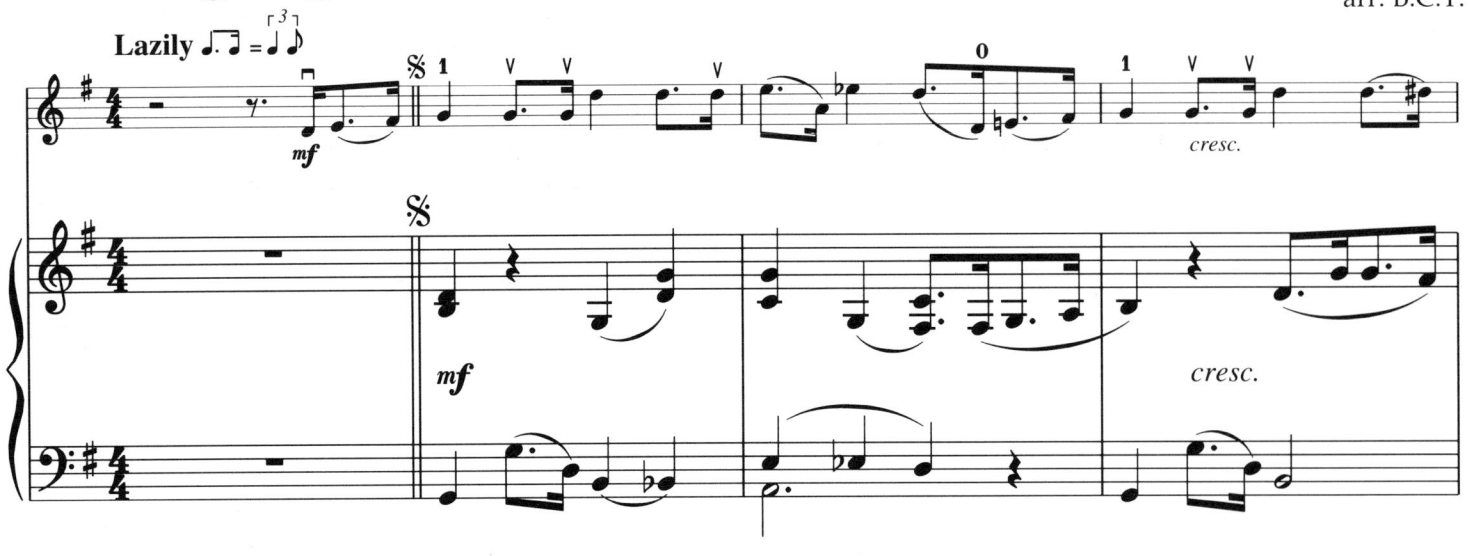

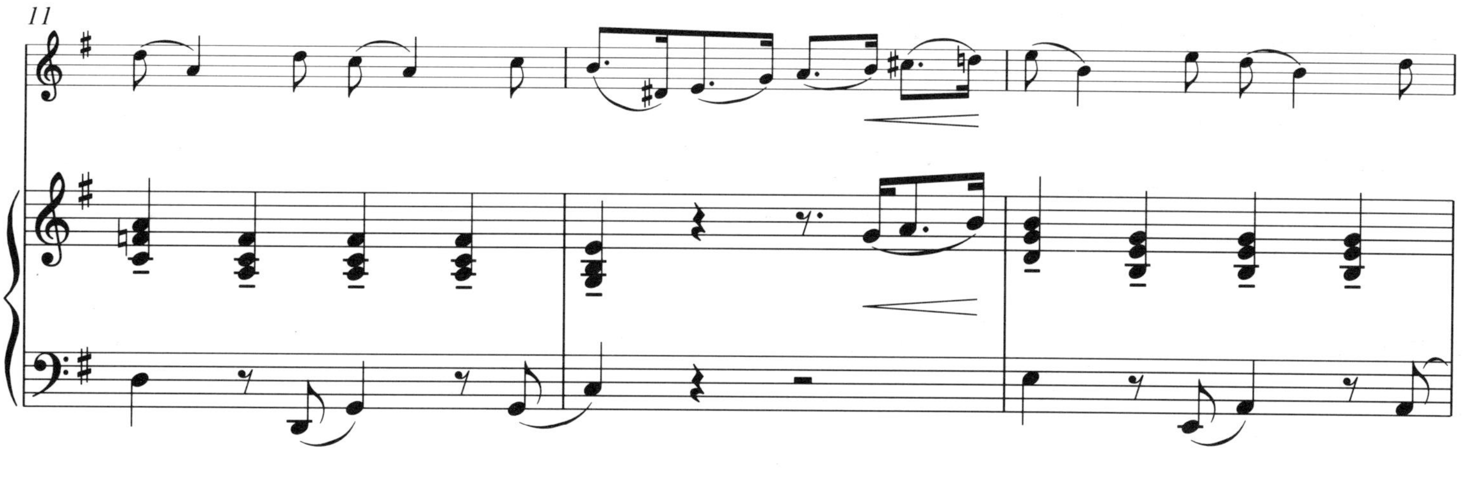
11

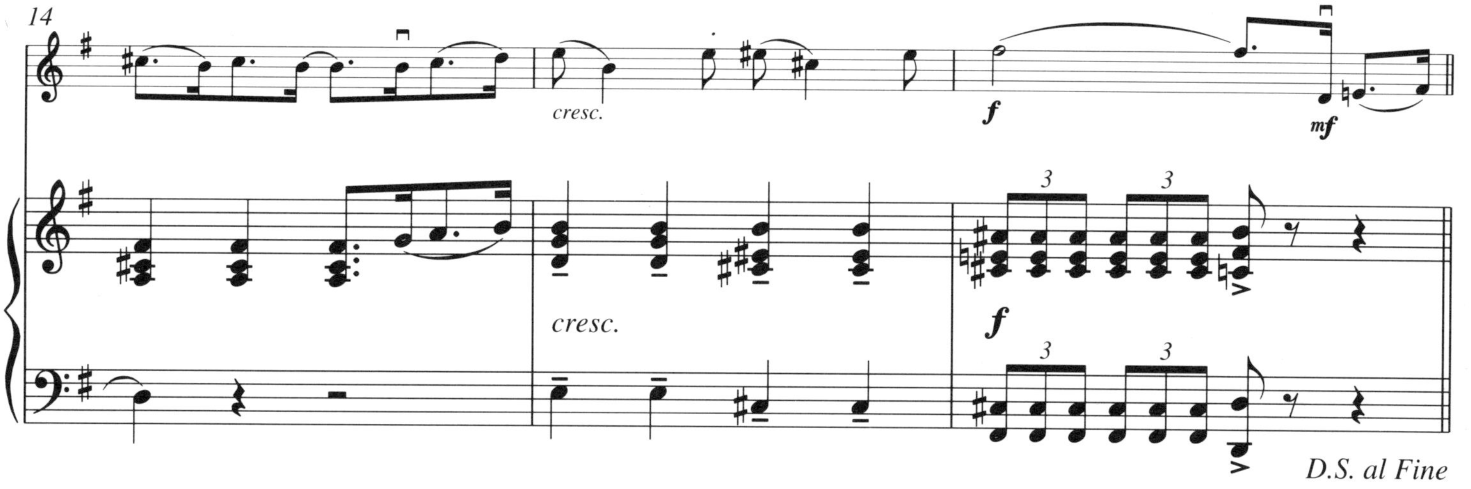
14
cresc.
f
mf
cresc.
f
D.S. al Fine

Menuet from *French Suite No. 3* (page 42)

J.S. Bach
arr. B.C.T.

Allegro non troppo

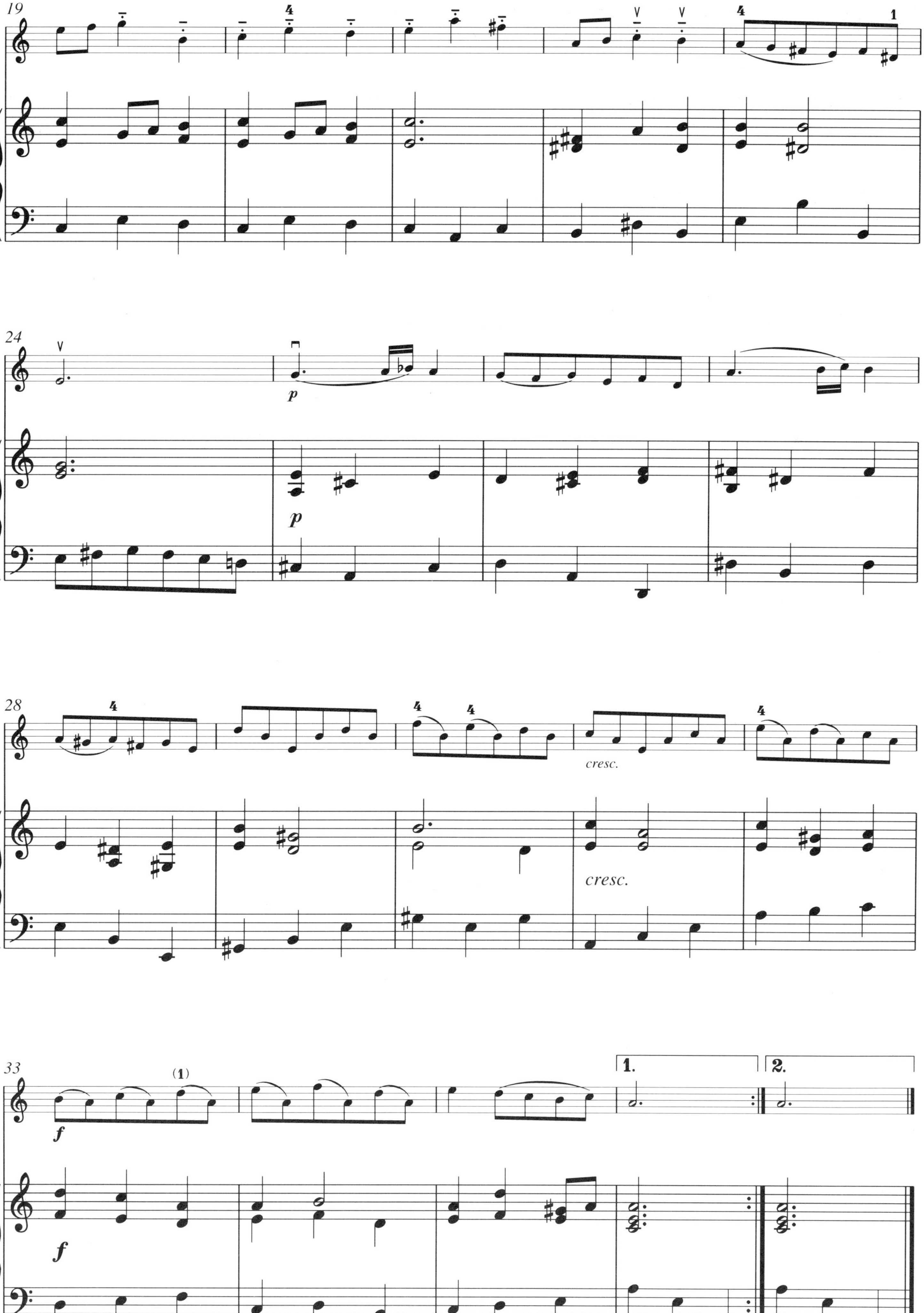
cresc.
cresc.

Sunshine hornpipe *(page 44)*

traditional Irish
arr. B.C.T.

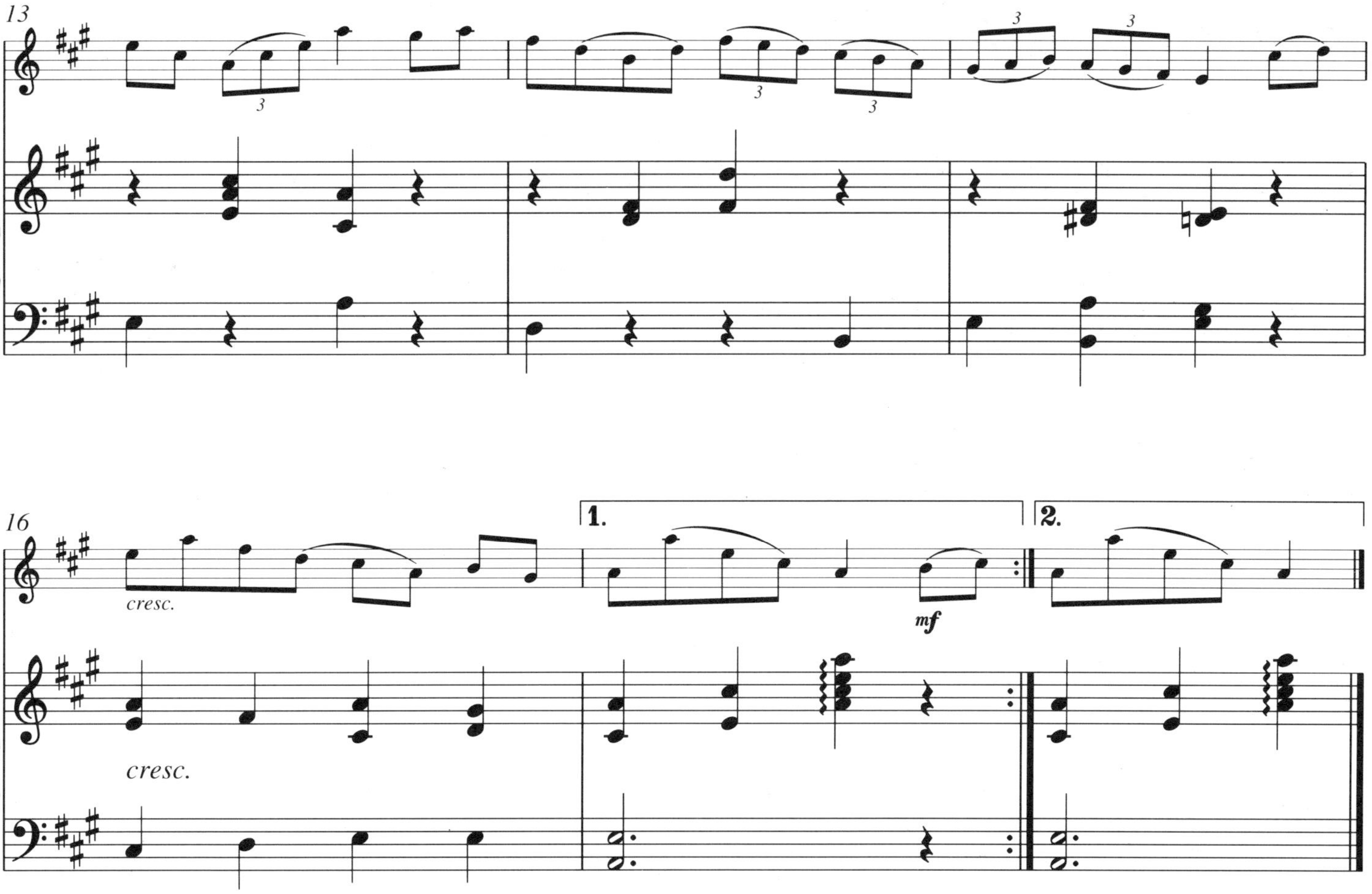
13
16
cresc.
cresc.
1.
2.
mf

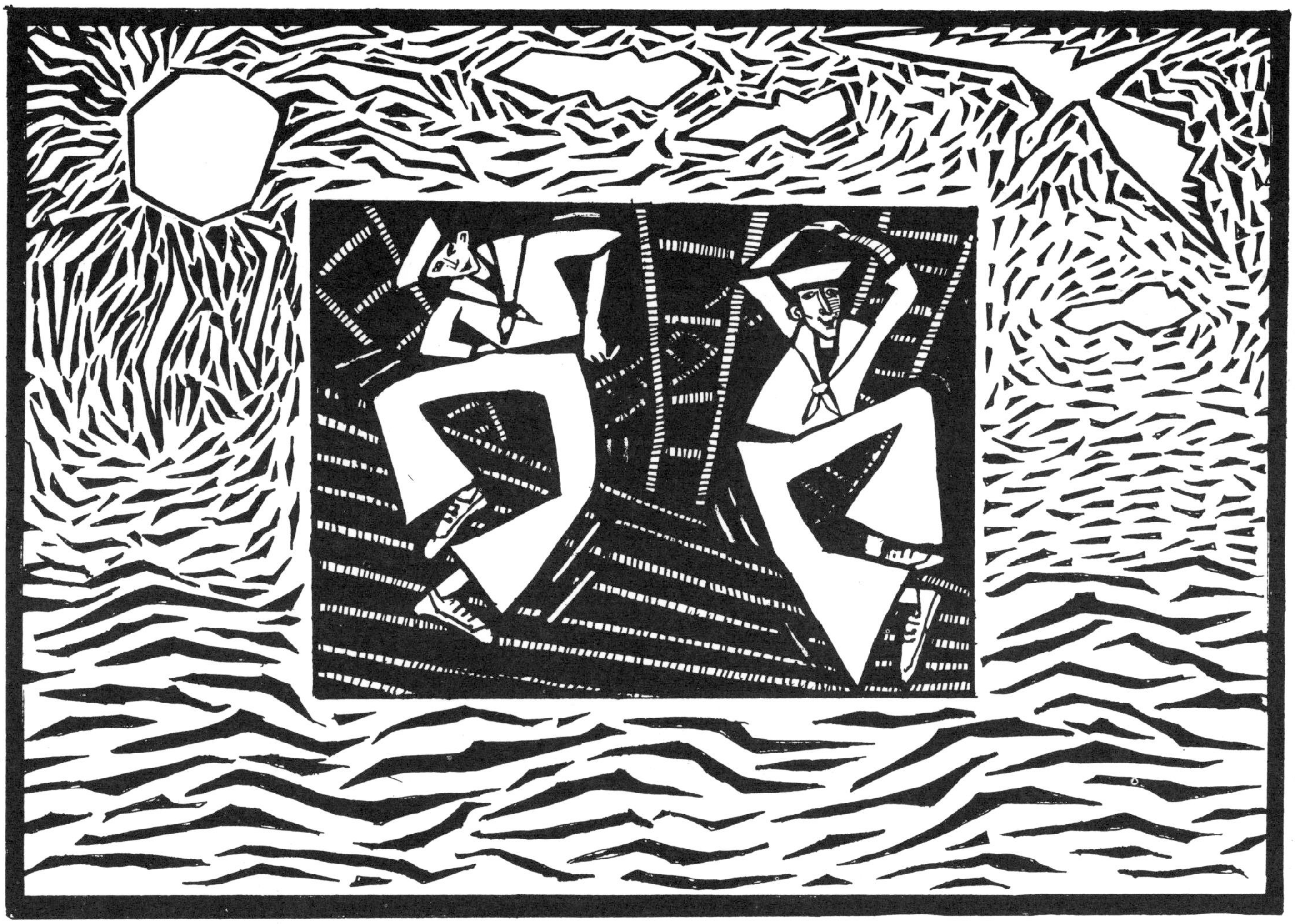

Where is love? *(page 44)*

Lionel Bart
arr. B.C.T.

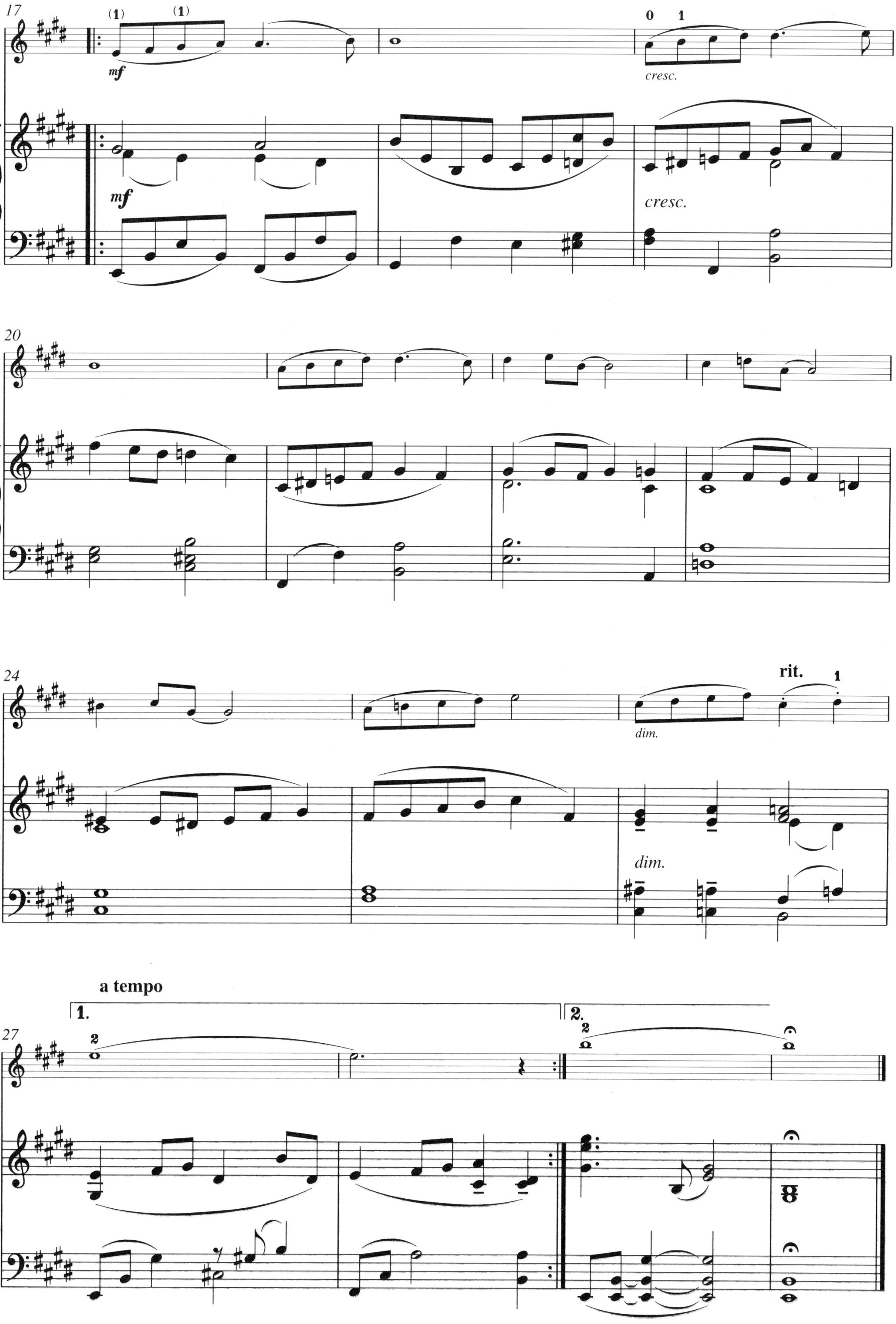
17
mf
cresc.
20
24
rit.
dim.
a tempo
1.
2.
27

Index

The page numbers in the Violin Part are given in brackets.

Agatha Christie's Poirot, 50 (39)
Amazing grace, 30 (29)
Bill Bailey, won't you please come home?, 24 (25)
Cossack song, 31 (29)
Dona nobis pacem (unaccompanied round), (11)
Down the green fields, 6 (8)
Duet from 12 Duos (unaccompanied duet), (35)
Duo in G (unaccompanied duet), (17)
Entr'acte *from* Rosamunde (No. 2), 18 (18)
Greensleeves, 16 (15)
Hard fact (unaccompanied round), (8)
Hava nagila, 23 (23)
How delightful to see (unaccompanied duet), (6)

Idylle, Op. 30 No. 1, 22 (23)
In dulci jubilo, 4 (6)
Jim Boulton's fancy, 21 (21)
La Cucaracha, 32 (30)
Little brown jug (unaccompanied duet), (5)
Londonderry air, 46 (37)
Mango walk (unaccompanied duet), (24)
Menuet *from* French Suite No. 3, 58 (42)
Minuet *from* Berenice, 36 (32)
Mirror canon (unaccompanied duet), (22)
Morris dance, 28 (27)
On wings of song, 40 (34)
Pillow dance (unaccompanied duet) from 44 Duos for Two Violins, (28)
Sailor's waltz, 26 (26)
Siciliano *from* Album for the Young, 54 (41)
Simple gifts, 8 (10)

Strange adventure (unaccompanied duet) from Yeoman of the Guard, (14)
Strangers in the night, 34 (31)
Sunshine hornpipe, 60 (44)
Swinging star, 56 (42)
The animals went in two by two, 20 (20)
The cuckoo (unaccompanied duet), (9)
The jolly miller, 17 (16)
The lonely goatherd, 47 (38)
The Mexican hat dance, 14 (13)
The mountains high, 38 (33)
The wraggle taggle gypsies, 3 (4)
The wreck *(round)*, 9 (10)
Theme and variations *from* The 'Surprise' Symphony, 12 (12)
Theme *from* Bergerac, 43 (36)
Trumpet hornpipe, 19 (19)
Tum balaika, 10 (11)
Turkey in the straw, 2 (4)

Waltz *from* Swan Lake, 52 (40)
Where is love?, 62 (44)

Acknowledgements

The author and publishers would like to thank Heather Fleck for her help in the preparation of this book.
Grateful thanks are due to the following who have contributed copyright material:

Jan Holdstock for 'Hard fact' and 'The wreck'

Lakeview Music Publishing Co Ltd for 'Where is love?' by Lionel Bart. © Lakeview Music Publishing Co Ltd. All rights reserved. Used by permission.

Hal Leonard Publishing Corporation for 'The Lonely Goatherd' (from 'The Sound of Music') Lyrics by Oscar Hammerstein II, Music by Richard Rodgers. Copyright © 1959 by Richard Rodgers and Oscar Hammerstein II. Copyright renewed. WILLIAMSON MUSIC owner of publication and allied rights throughout the world. International copyright secured. All Rights Reserved.

MCA Music Ltd for 'Strangers in the night' by Bert Kaempfert, Charles Singleton and Eddie Snyder. © 1966 Champion Music Corp/MCA Inc/Screen Gems EMI Music. International copyright secured. All rights reserved.

Shogun/Eaton Music Limited for 'Bergerac' by George Fenton. © 1981 Shogun/Eaton Music Limited.

Standard Music Ltd for 'Agatha Christie's Poirot' by Chris Gunning. © 1989 Standard Music Ltd, 1A Farm Place, London W8 7SX.

Universal Edition (London) Ltd for 'Pillow Dance' from Béla Bartók 44 Duos for 2 Violins. © Copyright 1933 by Universal Edition (London) Ltd. Copyright renewed 1960 by Boosey & Hawkes Inc. New York. Reproduced by permission. All rights reserved.

Every effort has been made to trace and acknowledge copyright owners. If any right has been omitted the publishers offer their apologies and will rectify this in subsequent editions following notification.

ISBN 0 7136 3729 3

First published 1993 by A & C Black (Publishers) Ltd, 35 Bedford Row, London WC1R 4JH
© 1993 A & C Black (Publishers) Ltd

Apart from any fair dealing for the purposes of research or private study, or criticism or review, as permitted under the Copyright, Designs and Patents Act, 1988, this publication may be reproduced, stored or transmitted, in any forms or by any means, only with the prior permission in writing of the publishers, or in the case of reprographic reproduction in accordance with the terms of licences issued by the Copyright Licensing Agency. Inquiries concerning reproduction outside those terms should be sent to the publishers at the above-mentioned address.

Music arranged by James Alexander (J.A), Barrie Carson Turner (B.C.T.), Heather Fleck (H.F.) and Jane Sebba (J.S.)
Illustrations by Dee Shulman
Cover by Alex Ayliffe
Music setting by Andrew Jones
Printed in Great Britain by St Edmundsbury Press, Bury St Edmunds, Suffolk